Assignments 3

PPY PRESS - LONDON

Published by the PPY PRESS
Press Photographers Year Ltd.
52-58 Shorts Gardens
London WC2H 9AN
call us: +44(0)20 3239 9908
email us: info@theppy.com
visit us: www.theppy.com

A catalogue record for this book is available from the British Library.

Produced by Tim Bishop and Dillon Bryden
Design: SMITH, Lesley Gilmour, Victoria Forrest
www.smith-design.com

Origination: Euro Digital, Passau
Printing: Passavia, Passau
Binding: Conzella, Pfarrkirchen
Printed in Germany on 170 gsm BVS matte
and 300gsm Invercote G acid-free papers.

ISBN 978-0-9556019-1-0

Assignments 3 romania joins eu, ban ki-moon, iphone , h5n1, comet mcnaught, cash for peerages, maddy, $2 to the £, sarkozy elected, paisley first minister, blair resigns, cutty sark fire, lewis in f1, star wars 30th, bombs in london, summer floods, alan johnston freed, federer's fifth wimbledon, russians expelled, final harry potter, scouting 100th, india's 60th anniversary, withdrawal from basra, menzies resigns, led zeppelin back, bhutto assassinated, analogue switch off, kenyan elections.

The Press Photographer's Year

I once won the top prize for news photography organised by a great camera manufacturer, and supported by my newspaper. I hadn't even entered it myself, but shrewdly this competition rewarded the printer, as well as the photographer, with quite large cash prizes. Our canny darkroom at The Times had dug out the neg, beautifully printed it up and submitted it for me. The first I knew I had actually won was a tip-off phone call from my picture editor. He knew I had won, because he was one of the judges.

Thrilled, I rang New York to tell the one photographer I most admired, a man whose ideas and thoughts not only shaped the way I thought of my own career, but whose own photography still now represents the very best of news work for a generation of photographers. A former long standing president of Magnum, I wanted him to know that after all his help and advice to me since we had met on my first major overseas assignment: I was on my way.

"Competitions are crap", he said.

Nearly twenty years later, when members of the British Press Photographers' Association (BPPA) came to form the ideas for a completely new competition that wouldn't be crap, I asked Philip Jones Griffiths to be our first Chairman of the Jury for The Press Photographers' Year (PPY). I didn't tell anyone, because I knew he would decline. And although he wasn't at all well, he was excited by what we were trying to do, and asked me to come over and see him.

The PPY would be all about putting 'photography' back into photographic competitions. We wanted to find the very best news images, we were not looking to crown a photographer, hail a best of best newspaper, or agency. This was to be a great record of the year, a lasting tribute. The competition designed for photographers by photographers. There would be not just a winner, there would be a book, a great exhibition.

When Philip's book 'Vietnam Inc' was published in 1971, it was seen as 'unpatriotic' but later it became one of the deciding factors in showing the American public just what was happening in 'Nam. His work was remarkable because he didn't so much as cover the war in Vietnam, as immerse himself in it. He told me that at one point he went for more than two years photographing the war without phoning anyone, least of all the picture desk at The Observer, who had assigned him.

Our Chairman, Clive Limpkin, published his own book about the same time, The Battle of the Bogside, which won him the Robert Capa Gold Medal. Twenty years later on assignment in Ulster, I was astonished to see the haunting image of a young boy in gas mask holding a petrol bomb that formed the cover of Clive's book, exactly reproduced in a mural painted onto the side wall of a terraced house in Londonderry.

Clive and the jury had before them a mammoth task of sorting a record entry of over seven and half thousand images: Colin Davey, founder member of the BPPA, and former 'Royal Photographer of the Year' with thirteen years on the Mail; Justin Sutcliffe, former winner of the World Press Photo Golden Eye award; Abbie Trayler- Smith, recently covering assignments in Iraq and the aftermath of the Asian tsunami for Oxfam, UNICEF, and The Observer magazine; Eddie Mulholland, vice-chair of the BPPA, and a previous PPY winner; Graham Harrison whose work spans the Telegraph magazine to photographing an award winning calendar for Shell; Bob Martin, whose many international awards include British Sports Photographer of the Year three times, and Sports Picture of the Year in World Press Photo who led the judging of the sports section with Chris Cole, formerly of The Times and Allsport, who himself has won Sports Picture of the Year three times.

This year we welcome Matt Beard, who within weeks of taking up his new role at Canon Cameras, immediately backed us to launch the competition for 2008. Without his support, and the backing of Canon, we would quite simply not exist.

And without John Langley and his assistant Alison Chown at the National Theatre, whose unfailing support right from the very start of the PPY has been a vital key to our growing success, Chris Kay and his team at Loxelys, our brilliant printers, and Tom Scott and James Crossett of Talking Pixels, who built our ground breaking website, we wouldn't have a competition either.

Once again Stu Smith, assisted by Lesley Gilmour and Victoria Forrest have brought that unique design stamp to both the book and the exhibition. And finally Alistair Mackeown and Brian Murphy have proved vital and longstanding supporters. We owe them all a huge vote of thanks.

Every aspect of how the competition functions, from how we communicate with our entrants, to how we get pictures on the wall, are the brainchild and execution of Dillon Bryden. He devotes huge amounts of time to a competition that he can never enter, let alone win.

Sadly, Philip Jones Griffiths never got to hear the news of this year's PPY, as he died on March 19th, leaving a huge gap in the ranks of those who really care about championing great news photography.

Philip said: "Be honest in how you select, and let the honest images shine through".

tim bishop
co-founder of the press photographer's year

contents

daniel berehulak GETTY IMAGES

Former Pakistani premier Benazir Bhutto adjusts her headscarf during a press conference at her house in Karachi, Pakistan. Bhutto held prayers for those killed in the deadly suicide attack on her homecoming parade. Bhutto had returned three days before after eight years of self-imposed exile. She blamed Islamist militants for carrying out the bombing where 139 people were killed. October 21st 2007.

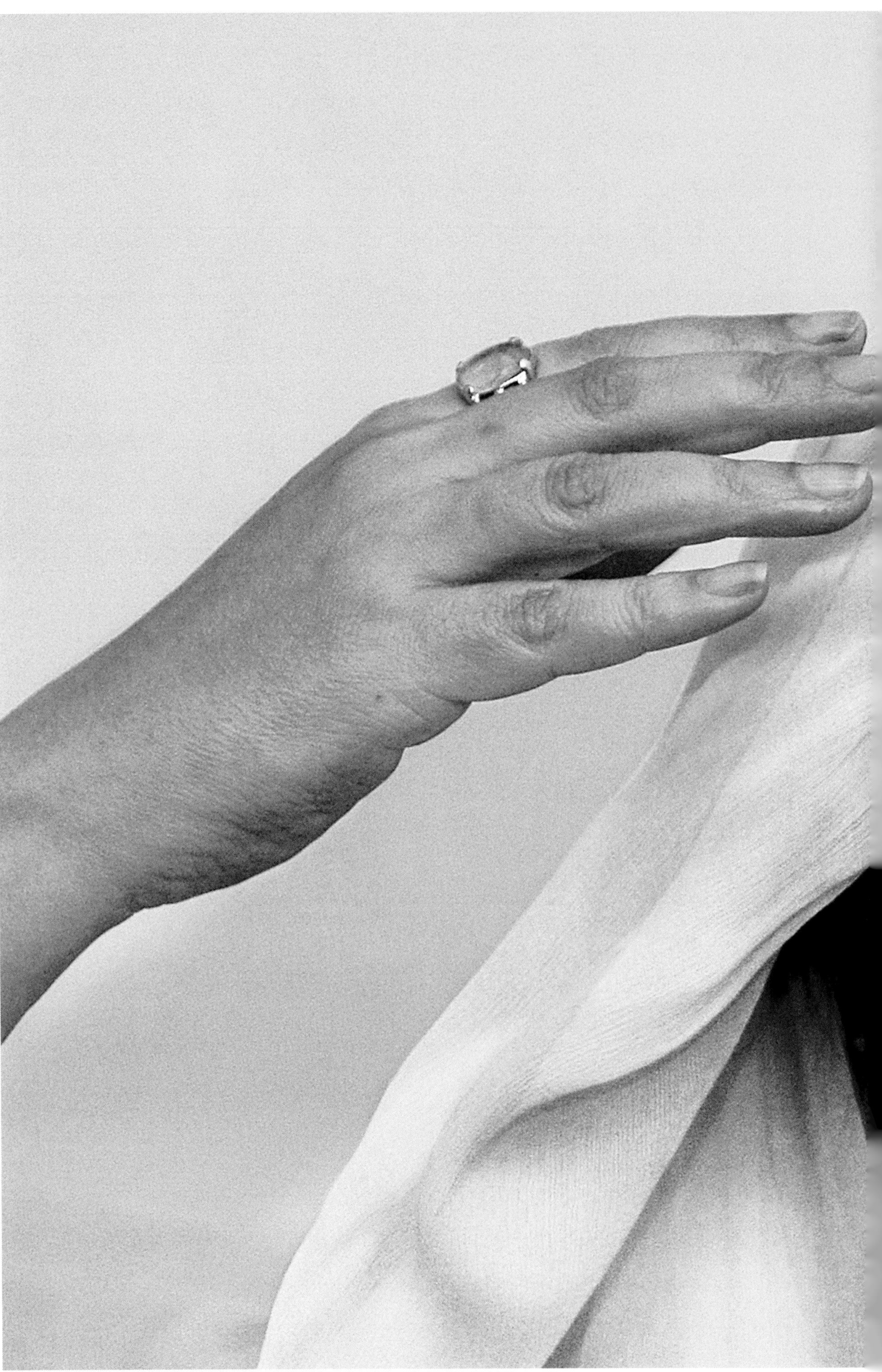

first, the bad news...

clive limpkin chairman of the 2008 jury

First, the bad news...

The well-respected, well-paid British press photographer is an endangered species if not a dying breed, under siege as never before.

As salaries, shifts, day rates, expenses, and repro fees decline in real terms, assignments per day and pressures increase, copyrights are surrendered as a term of employment, job security dissolves, work is restricted by the fear of child pornography, terrorism or abuse of civil liberties, and 'citizen journalism' becomes a synonym for cheap rates. Videos will soon offer useable still grabs, plunging the press photographer into a world of multi-tasking much loved by accountants but best judged by listening to the musical rendition of a one-man band. (Sadly, my cardiologist forbids me to raise the subject of by-lines).

The media world changes so fast it is difficult to generalise or forecast the state of play, but here are random news snippets appearing the day this was written...

- Austin Mitchell gathers support of 190 MPs for a motion permitting photography in public places in the hope of reducing hindrance by police and security personnel.
- Proposed US legislation on 'orphan work' (data whose owner or originator cannot be traced), that would legitimise copyright abuse is being considered by the European Union.
- The same EU announces a 'Cultures on my Street' photo competition which is 'as easy as a grabbing your camera and stepping outside the front door'. Well, not quite: small-print rules reveal participants must prove all subjects have posed voluntarily, whilst their handy online model release form insists the photographs can be used free by the EU 'without limitation in space or time'. Best stay indoors.
- By extrapolating newspaper circulation decline in the US and the growth of internet news hits, it has been estimated that the last copy an American newspaper will land on a front porch around 2043. My guess is only TV will be there to record the event.
- Footballer Wayne Rooney's fiancée, Colleen McLoughlin, describes herself as a 'journalist' on the wedding banns (based on her £100,000 'lifestyle' column in Closer magazine), while Wayne puts down 'proffesional footballer' [*sic*] - the happy couple are set to reap a reputed £3.2 million from OK magazine for exclusive rights.

The good news is that, despite the above, 325 British press photographers entered 7,500 photographs in this year's competition for no cash reward but merely to showcase their talents - not only for their peers but also for the public whose generic image of the profession is probably that of a melee walking backwards into lamp-posts ahead of Britney Spears.

But that's celeb-led Britain for you. While Arles, Perpignan, Toronto, Madrid and now New York host International Photographic Festivals, we inaugurate a Young Photographers Award co-sponsored by Hello! magazine. God, how we need The Press Photographer's Year. Yet its future rests on the shoulders of just two men, Tim Bishop and Dillon Bryden, who, despite full-time careers in photography, spend three months a year keeping the project alive, coupled with the essential sponsorship of Canon, and input from members of the BPPA.

So why should they be struggling to raise the profile of the profession and maintain sponsorship in Britain, while across the narrow Channel there's a nation with a different concept of press photography and respect for the practitioners and in America they're happy to stump up $450 million for the Newseum of Journalism in Washington D.C.?

There's no simple answer, nor to the question of the PPY's way forward in raising press photography's profile, but my brainstorming penn'orth on the latter would centre on participation and accessibility:

Having produced a website of model clarity, how about introducing a People's Choice category by asking the public to vote online for their winner from the finalists (Sony's inaugural World Photography Awards website had 68 million hits), plus exhibition visitors also choosing electronically?

The National Theatre is an undeniably prestigious venue, but you can't beat open-air access. Paris's Assemblee Nationale proudly displays photo exhibitions on their railings and while I'm not suggesting the House of Commons might play ball, why shouldn't the exhibition share the Green Park railings with the present tat art, or be projected in the evening on buildings?

My son went to Tate Modern and asked why they weren't treating 3D Animation as an art; as a result he's curating an annual two-day seminar there on the subject. Should I send him round with a copy of this book?

As for my opinion of individual pictures, you'll never know. Why do the visual arts attract such verbosity, trying to explain pictures? Sure, there are column inches to be filled and critics' children must eat, but do we need more than the picture itself and a description of its origins to judge it? A photo either grabs you or it doesn't - we don't need an expert's verbiage to explain, you are the expert. That's what this book and the exhibition are for. (It's probably an appropriate moment whilst dabbing froth from my lips to mention the Chairman's opinions are not necessarily those of fellow-jurors, the British Press Photographers' Association or the sponsors). Which brings us to the judging...

It's been a chest-beating, hand-wringing year of judging the judging, when two London-based photographers, part of this year's World Press Photo jury, broke the fifty-one-year juror's oath of silence (perr-lease, we're not picking a Pope here) to ask if we really needed to see more and more suffering in the entries; the overall winning image, Tim Hetherington's fatigued soldier, typifies the current vogue for bleak news photography.

Sadly, both the two jurors and Hetherington write in the style of a Media Studies thesis - do we really need Brechtian quotes or use the word 'decontextualisation'? Come on lads, we're trying to make photography more accessible.

A valid point was raised, though, when the jury was shown a photo of people taking snaps with their phones. Was it a wedding or a film premiere? With a sub-jury whittling the finalists down to 17,000 (!) there was no time for captions. It proved to be an Iranian public execution, information that transformed the image. In London, we had no captions either but during the initial slide show, in which every picture was viewed by the jury, a caption would be read out if we asked for more detail. A print of every picture was then laid out at the National Theatre for our re-consideration, unlike in Amsterdam, where photos were flashed up and jurors voted by pressing a button in the darkness attached to a computer originally used for a Dutch TV game show.

It was at this point our disparate views emerged, and what we shall call 'persuasions' aired with varied intensity, tensions occasionally simmering close to the surface like separated couples meeting on Access Sunday. No blows were struck, discipline being maintained by kindness alone.

At one stage it was pointed out that after listening to a succession of speechlets, I'd changed my mind three times about a category winner - thank God a casting vote was never needed. Suffice to say, I found the overall quality superb, the jury's choice inspiring, and the judging a joy.

Having moved to travel photography and spent the previous year in India for a gentile photographic book, the occasion brought back glorious memories of the adrenaline rush and sheer thrill of nailing a picture out of nothing, the magic of the profession at its best, and why it really stays in the blood forever. The 325 entrants may be suffering for their art in today's climate, but there is no profession in the world to match it.

sean smith THE GUARDIAN
US army medics attached to a Stryker Brigade Combat Team of 2nd Infantry (named after the eight-wheeled Stryker combat vehicles they travel in) attend to a badly wounded Iraqi soldier in Karradah, near Ameriyah, a Sunni neighbourhood in west Baghdad, an area allegedly controlled by Al-Qaeda. The US soldiers heard an explosion in a house that they suspected was a homemade bomb factory. It turned out the bombmaker had accidentally blown themselves up. While searching the neighbouring properties a second explosion occured that injured a passing Iraqi army patrol that too had responded to the initial blast. Some local people were also injured, and treated by the Americans. 30th May 2007.

sean smith THE GUARDIAN
A US soldier attached to a Stryker Brigade Combat Team of 2nd Infantry takes a break in an Iraqi army post in Ameriyah, a neighbourhood of west Baghdad allegedly controlled by Al-Qaeda whilst an Iraqi soldier performs his midday prayers. 26th May 2007.

sean smith THE GUARDIAN
A company of US soldiers from a Stryker Brigade Combat Team of 2nd Infantry had tried to stop a car that had passed them a few times, and they thought was suspicious. They fired warning shots but then opened fired on the car when it failed to stop. The driver was killed and the body was dragged into the house of a nearby lady who remonstrated with the soldiers for their actions. It seems that he was just a local taxi driver. Baghdad, Iraq. 22nd May 2007.

 THE GUARDIAN
US Soldiers attached to a Stryker Brigade Combat Team of 2nd Infantry post lookout from an Iraqi army post in Ameriyah, a Sunni neighbourhood in west Baghdad. US troops regularly visit the Iraqi positions to gather intelligence, and to provide support to the Iraqis. 18th May 2007.

sean smith THE GUARDIAN
US soldiers attached to a Stryker Brigade Combat Team of 2nd Infantry provide cover from possible sniper fire as other soldiers try to put out the fire in one of their Bradley armored vehicles. It was hit by an I.E.D. moments before in Amiriyah a Sunni neighborhood in west Baghdad allegedly controlled by Al-Qaeda. Despite being the first on the scene there was nothing they could do to save the seven occupants. 19th May 2007.

first prize: live news

andrew parsons PRESS ASSOCIATION
Soldiers from the Worcester and Sherwood Foresters regiment move Private Davey Graham, 21, from Nottingham, to a waiting helicopter by makeshift stretcher so he can be medivaced out of the Green zone in Helmand province, Southern Afghanistan after he was shot in an ambush by the Taliban. 14th August 2007.

philip coburn

Soldiers of the British Reconnaissance Force firing on the Taliban compound at Musa Quala in Helmand Province, Afghanistan. Members of 52 Brigade, 4/73 Battery Area Special Observational Unit are a rapid fighting force used against the Taliban in Helmand Province. The BRF had recently cleared a secure route for a 400 vehicle convoy intent on retaking the Taliban stronghold of Musa Quala. Their task during the resulting battle was to co-ordinate air strikes and the use of fire-power in support of US troops. Over the course of this operation the BRF undertook the longest desert patrol since the Second World War. 10th December 2007.

john d mchugh

US soldiers from Able Troop, 3/71 Cav, 10th Mountain Division, take up defensive positions after an air assault by Chinook Helicopter to Barg-e-Matal village in Nuristan Province, Afghanistan. Following their first visit a month earlier, this five day operation began with a surprise landing, followed by the troops setting up a temporary base outside the village. Over the next four days senior commanders met with local leaders to discuss a variety of security and reconstruction issues. This is the furthest north that US troops have pushed: "further than the Soviets ever got" is their proud claim. 27th April 2007.

lefteris pitarakis AP
The aftermath of the two explosions that went off near the truck carrying Pakistan's former Prime Minister Benazir Bhutto, in Karachi, Pakistan. She survived the attack but at least 140 people were killed. 18th October 2007.

lefteris pitarakis AP
People try to help the bomb victims moments after the two explosions targeted former Prime Minister Benazir Bhutto's homecoming parade, Karachi, Pakistan. 18th October 2007.

daniel berehulak GETTY IMAGES
Injured men lay on the floor of a Karachi hospital after an apparent suicide car bomb blast was detonated near a vehicle carrying former Pakistani Prime Minister Benazir Bhutto during a homecoming welcome in Karachi, Pakistan. Over one hundred people are reported dead with many more injured. Hundreds of thousands of people turned out to greet the former Prime Minister after her return from eight years of self imposed exile. 19th October 2007.

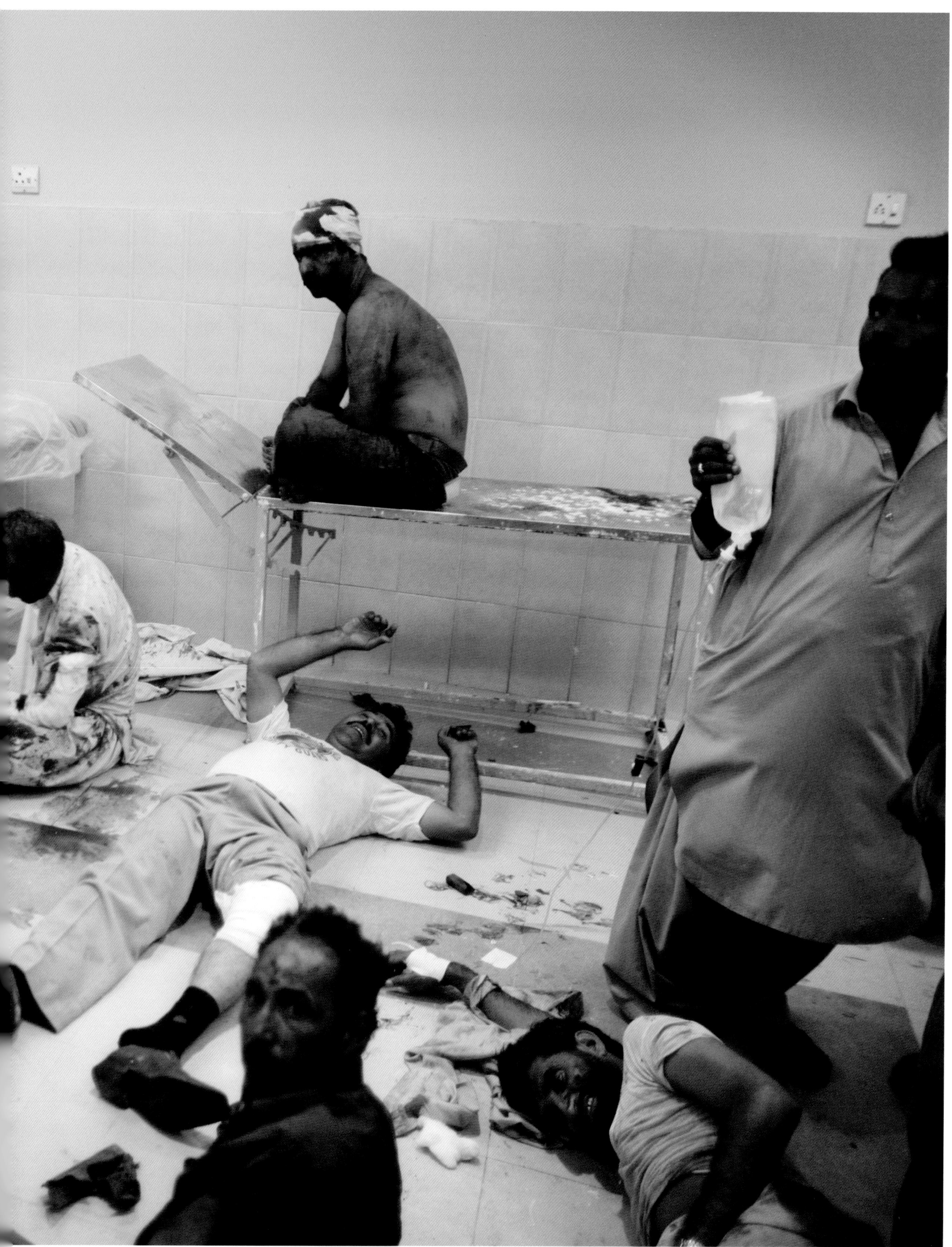

james veysey CAMERA PRESS
A wrestling competition in Bint Jbeil, Lebanon, a year after the town was heavily damaged during the 34-day conflict between Israel and Hezbollah. The "Biggest International Competition for the Free Professional Wrestling" is organised by the Lebanese Sporting Club of Bint Jbeil, a social, non-political club. 25th August 2007.

stuart griffiths
Calvalryman Andy Anthony Julien was victim to a friendly fire incident when a British Army Challenger tank fired upon his Challenger tank, five days into the war in Iraq. 10th June 2007

OAN
BOTEZĂTOR
POCĂITIVĂ
POCĂITIVĂ
CĂ S'A APRO-
IAT ÎMPĂRĂ-
IA CERURI-
OR

david bebber THE TIMES
Local residents take part in the Saturday of the Dead ceremony held in the Orthodox church in the village of Matau in Romania where the traditional way of life may be under threat from EU legislation. 9th February 2007.

david bebber THE TIMES
Shepherd Ion Sulca (left) prepares to pour a cup of plum schnapps at his home in the village of Matau, Romania where the traditional way of life may be under threat from EU legislation. 7th February 2007.

david bebber THE TIMES
Ion Visoiu feeds his cattle in the village of Matau, Romania. 7th February 2007.

david bebber THE TIMES
Ion Lupascu at home in the village of Matau, Romania. 9th February 2007.

david bebber THE TIMES
Ion and Maria Lupascu at home in the village of Matau, Romania. 8th February 2007.

david bebber THE TIMES
Ion Visoiu feeds his sheep with willow branches in the village of Matau, Romania. 7th February 2007.

andrew mcconnell

The Xabaalaha Shanad camp for displaced persons in the center of Hargeisa, Somaliland. The camp is one of many around the capital which house the thousands of people who fled to Ethiopia during the civil war in 1988 and returned in 1991. Although Somaliland has been stable for 16 years poverty and unemployment are widespread and the government hopes international recognition will provide much needed financial support. 28th July 2007.

following spread

carol allen storey

Ayubu is 2 years old and an AIDS orphan cared for by his uncle Abel,14, also an AIDS orphan. Horrendous lesions have stripped skin away from Ayubu's bottom, an opportunistic skin disorder derived from the AIDS virus. He is being treated topically with honey to alleviate the suffering. Keko Village, Tanzania. 14th November 2007.

luca ferrari PROSPEKT

A woman after the Eid-ul Fitr prayer (that marks the end of Ramadan) at the central mosque of Jolo city. For thirty years in the deep south of Philippines, different Muslim rebel groups have been fighting against the Government of Manila for the independence of their ancestral domain: Bangsamoro. The most important rebel group is the Moro Islamic Liberation Front (MILF). MILF, despite accusations to be linked with Abu Sayaff Group and Al-Qaeda, has strong support from the Muslim people (which represent the 5% of the entire population of the Philippines) concentrated in the island of Mindanao and Sulu archipelago. 11th October 2007.

leon mcgowran

Darren Liddle, a city trader, committed suicide by leaping from the 19th floor of the Hilton Hotel, Park Lane, London. An inquest into his death heard that he was driven to suicide by the pressures of work. 21st September 2007.

brian david stevens

"They that are left..." From a series of portraits of war veterans taken on Remembrance Sunday over the past five years. Inspired by the war poet Laurence Binyon's 'The Fallen', the portraits represent the faces of "unknown soldiers" and show no rank, insignia or medals. Instead they are faces only, each deep-etched with who they are and what they did, that we might look, and think - and thank them. 11th November 2007.

nic dunlop PANOS PICTURES

A Burmese soldier forming part of a security detail for a VIP visit to the Shwedagon Pagoda in Rangoon, Burma. 15th March 2007.

following spread

nic dunlop PANOS PICTURES

Armed Forces Day in the new Burmese capital of Nay Pyi Daw, central Burma. 15,000 soldiers paraded in an annual event that is recognised as the day the modern Burma army was founded. Nay Pyi Daw is 300 kilometres north of Rangoon. 27th March 2007.

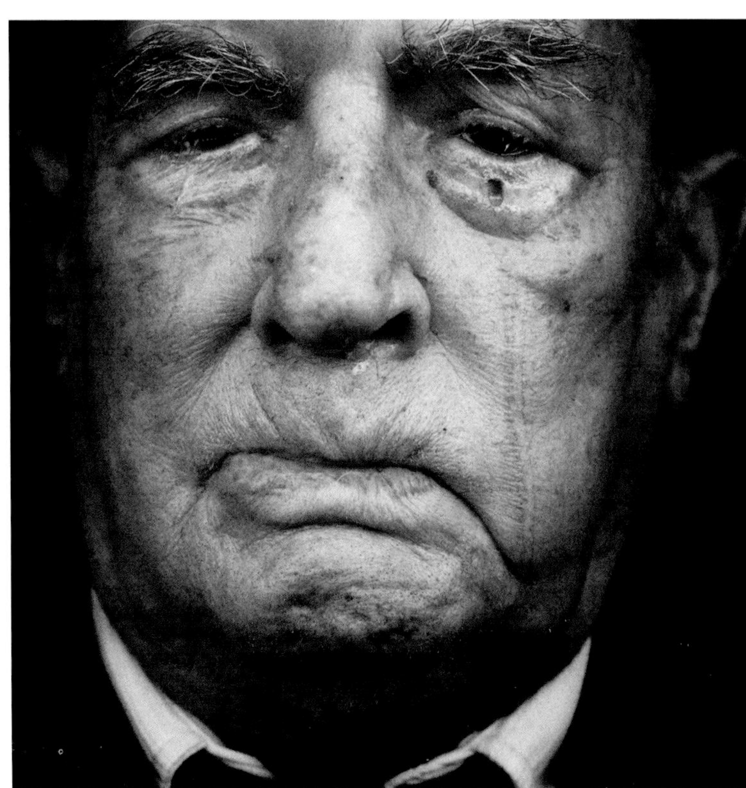

charles mcquillan PACEMAKER PRESS
Cathal McElhill carries the coffin of his nephew, nine-month old 'Baby James' after a funeral mass at the Sacred Heart Church in Omagh, Northern Ireland, for seven members of the same family who perished in a house fire. Post mortem examinations showed that 39-year-old Arthur McElhill, his 30-year-old partner Lorraine McGovern and their five children, aged between nine months and 13 years, died of smoke inhalation in the house fire at Lammy Crescent. Forensic tests revealed that petrol was sprinkled inside the house and then set alight. A murder investigation was launched and Arthur McElhill is believed to started the fire deliberately. 1st December 2007.

teri pengilley
Kate McCann, holding "Cuddles the Cat", fiddles with a Find Madeleine bracelet nearly 100 days after her four year old daughter was taken from their holiday apartment in Praia da Luz, Portugal. 3rd August 2007.

cathal mcnaughton PRESS ASSOCIATION
The British jury from the Coroner's inquest into the deaths of Diana, Princess of Wales and Dodi Al Fayed enter the Pont de l'Alma tunnel in Paris, France, where the Mercedes the couple were travelling in crashed had ten years earlier. The 11 jurors also visited the Ritz Hotel to see where the couple dined on the night they died. 8th October 2007.

bruno vincent
Former butler to Diana, Princess of Wales Paul Burrell poses for a photograph on the steps of the Royal Courts of Justice in London. 14th January 2007.

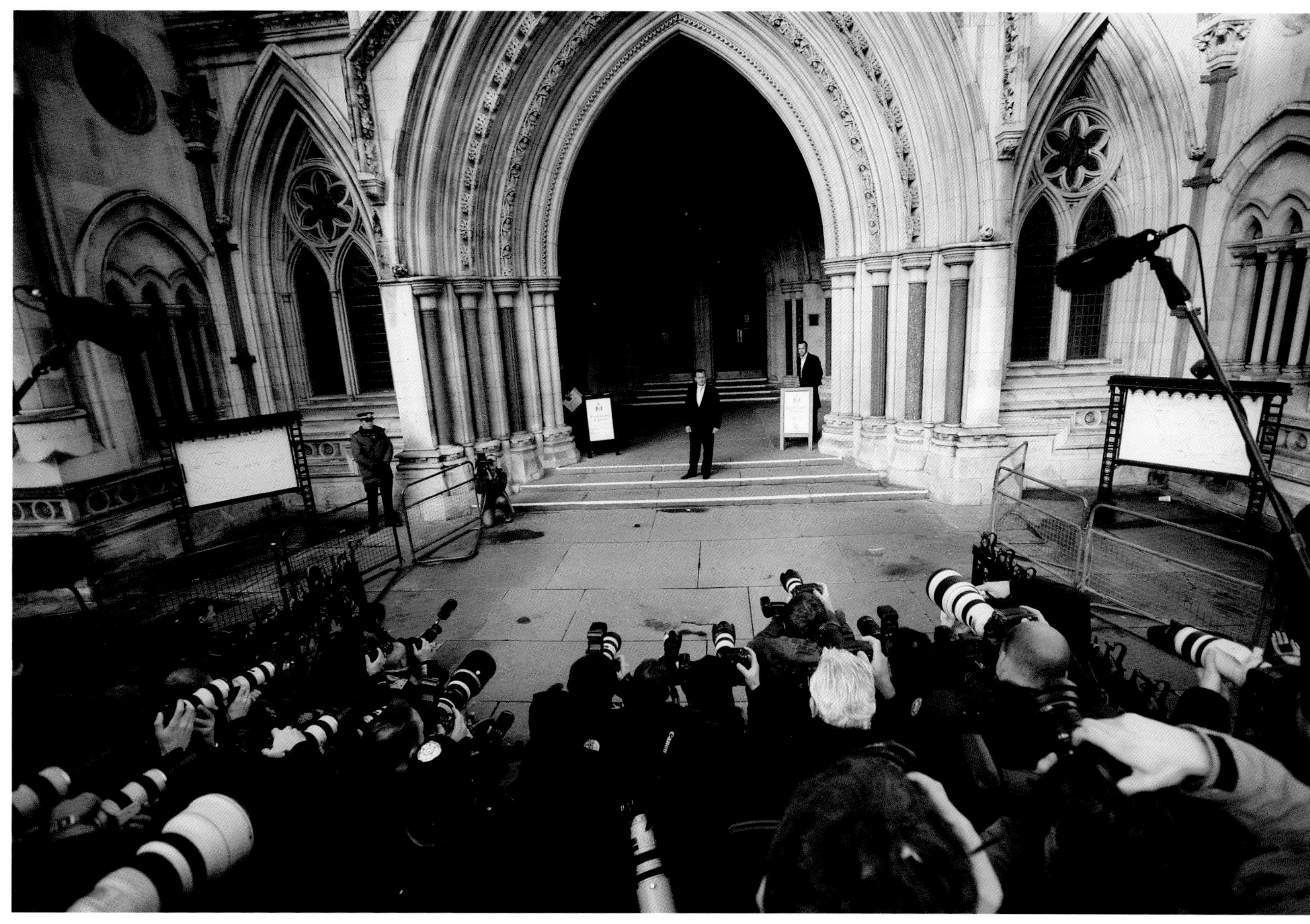

first prize: news folio of the year

daniel berehulak GETTY IMAGES

The town of Tewkesbury is pictured surrounded by water, as large areas of Gloucestershire, England, flooded following torrential rain. Flash flooding caused severe disruption across the UK. 22nd July 2007.

matt cardy

Norman Aitken surveys the damage to his home after it was flooded by the rise in the level of the River Severn in Gloucester, England. 24th July 2007.

david levene

Scavengers search the beach early in the morning three days after the MSC Napoli container vessel was beached at Branscombe Bay in Devon, England, after sustaining damage during a storm in the English Channel. The vessel shed around 100 of its containers into the waters at Branscombe, the contents of which continued to wash up onto the shore for days. People travelled from around the country following reports that expensive items, such motorbikes and car parts, were being salvaged from the containers on the beach. 23rd January.

james boardman

Some of the 5,260 tonnes of timber lost when the Greek-registered Ice Prince went down off Portland Bill is washed up on Worthing beach in West Sussex, England. 20th January 2008.

zak waters

From a series called 'Birdmen', an insight into the diminishing world of Pigeon Racing in the UK. One of the Birdmen in his Poly Tunnel where he grows leeks, tomatoes and the like. Quite a number of the Birdmen in the North East grow their own vegetables next to their bird lofts. Tindale Crescent, near Bishop Auckland, County Durham, England. 15th February 2007.

brian david stevens

From the series "Doggerland", named after the former landmass in the southern North Sea which connected the island of Great Britain to mainland Europe during the last ice age. These pictures are the photographer's visual diary, documenting how he sees the world, and about his relationship with his surroundings. City of London. June to July 2007.

nigel dickinson

A worker recycling rubbish at night at "Smokey Mountain" the municipal rubbish dump at Steung Mean Chey, Phnom Penh, Cambodia. Smokey Mountain is notorious as more than 600 young children work there with 2000 adults recycling the city's rubbish, dumped by garbage trucks every day. People eat and sleep overnight in the rubbish and fumes. They work 24 hours a day, with headlamps at night, (the workers rent lamps and batteries for 1000 Rial, 25c in US$) collecting plastic, metals, wood, cloth & paper, which they sort and clean, weigh and sell, to be carried away for recycling. A day's work typically brings less than a dollar per person. The overpowering, acrid odour of grey smokey fumes blows across the dump, from which the place gets its name. 28th February 2007.

sean smith THE GUARDIAN
US Soldiers attached to a Stryker Brigade Combat Team of 2nd Infantry searching a mosque in Ameriyah, a Sunni neighbourhood of west Baghdad allegedly controlled by Al Qaeda. All they found was this boy, locked in a toilet after being held by local Sunni militia men, who claimed he was Al Qaeda. Ist May 2007.

nigel dickinson

A boy walks on the tracks from school on the outskirts of Phnom Penh. The journey from Phnom Penh to Battambang is the last working passenger route on Royal Cambodian Railways and only runs at weekends. A Czech made diesel locomotive leaves the capital Saturday morning, arriving in Battambang 22 hours later in the dead of night, and returns on Sunday. Max speed is about 30kmh, often slower due to the track's terrible condition. Carriages are dilapidated, with holes in the floor and only spaces for windows. Passengers sit or sleep on hardwood bench seats, hammocks, or on the floor of cargo carriages. The drivers, controllers & guards add to their small monthly pay by charging for local passengers and cargo; from motorbikes and local produce to timber loaded aboard at the 30 stations along the route. This together with other trains and farm vehicles further slows the journey. In rural areas, the track is a lifeline, and used for local transport on 'bamboo trains' powered by belt-motors. Boom towns, with a 'goldrush mentality' near the rapidly depleted rainforest, are a hive of activity, with logging as their resource. In the city, the railway has a life of its own, where people live and work nearby or on the track itself. Market stalls, restaurants, chairs and tables, are removed only briefly, when the infrequent train passes. 27th February 2007.

nigel dickinson
A fast-food mobile vendor selling snacks and drinks, as night approaches. Smokey Mountain, Steung Mean Chey, Phnom Penh, Cambodia. 28th February 2007.

andrew mcconnell
Children carry basins containing salt removed from the pans at Lake Katwe, Uganda. The salt will be piled high on the shore and shovelled into 100kg bags before being transported away on trucks. Many children do not attend school in order to work at the lake and earn income for their families, such as the children in this picture, all siblings, who work their family salt pan almost every day during the dry season. 28th December 2007.

timothy allen AXIOM

Ladakhi people and Buddhist monks walking down the mountain from Diskyit Monastery after The Dalai Lama gave Buddhist teachings to a crowd of thousands in the mountains near Diskyid Monastery, Nubra Valley, Leh Ladakh, India. 27th August 2007.

nigel dickinson

A man washes plastic bags in a water hole in the middle of "Smokey Mountain" the municipal rubbish dump at Steung Mean Chey, Phnom Penh, Cambodia. The clean plastic is sent for recycling. 28th February 2007.

first prize: news

peter macdiarmid GETTY IMAGES
People gather at the Australian War Memorial at Hyde Park Corner in London. The yearly ANZAC memorial service remembers the soldiers of Australia and New Zealand who fought in the two World Wars and came into being after the heroic campaign that followed the landings at ANZAC Cove in Gallipoli on April 25, 1915 in which the Allies lost 50,000 casualties in their battle with Turkish forces. The new memorial is engraved with 24,000 names of the hometowns of Australian men and women who served in the two World Wars. Superimposed on these place names are 47 battle sites representing some of the major theatres of war where Australians served. 25th April 2007.

following spread

dan chung THE GUARDIAN
Tony Blair boards the steps to his plane bound for home after his last official to meet George Bush. Washington D.C, USA. 18th May 2007.

cathal mcnaughton PRESS ASSOCIATION
HRH Queen Elizabeth II shelters from the rain at the official opening of the Lawn Tennis Association's new state of the art training facility in Roehampton, South West London. 29th March 2007.

VILLERS-BRETONNEUX
TOBRUK

steve parsons PRESS ASSOCIATION
Queen Elizabeth II with the current holders of the Order of Merit, at Buckingham Palace, London. A rather camera shy Lucian Freud turns away as the shutter fires. The order, established in 1902, is a reward for distinguished service in the armed forces, science, art, literature of for the promotion of culture, and is limited to the Sovereign and 24 members. 11th October 2007.

jeff j mitchell GETTY IMAGES
Gordon Brown addresses Labour party members at The Bridgewater Hall, Manchester, after being confirmed as the new Labour party leader and therefore the next Prime Minister of Great Britain. The 56-year-old Brown moved into No. 10 Downing Street in June that year when out-going Prime Minister Tony Blair stepped down from his 10 year reign as Labour Party Leader. 24th June 2007.

Long live
the king?
The Big Smoke

tom stoddart GETTY IMAGES FOR TIME MAGAZINE
A thoughtful Gordon Brown travels to the launch of his 'Gordon Brown for Britain' Prime Ministerial campaign, surrounded by morning rush hour commuters on London Underground's Piccadilly Line. 10th May 2007.

following spread

leon neal AGENCE FRANCE PRESSE
HRH Queen Elizabeth II walks into the House of Commons during the State Opening of Parliament. 6th November 2007.

ben gurr THE TIMES
Boris Johnson, the Conservative candidate for the Mayor of London, travels to a Tory Mayoral hustings in London on a Routemaster bus. 10th September 2007.

anthony devlin PRESS ASSOCIATION
Camilla, Duchess of Cornwall, visits a local butcher during a visit to the village of Bromham in Wiltshire. 17th July 2007.

dan chung THE GUARDIAN
Tony Blair flies back to Baghdad airport from the Green Zone in a Puma helicopter with armed escort. Baghdad, Iraq. 19th May 2007.

niall carson PRESS ASSOCIATION
DUP Leader Dr. Ian Paisley pictured during a pre-election interview in his Ballymena constituency. 20th February 2007.

rui vieira PRESS ASSOCIATION
A group of Muslim woman greet the media on Strafford Road, Spark Hill, Birmingham. Eight people had earlier been arrested under the Terrorism Act following raids on a number of local addresses. 31st January 2007.

dylan martinez REUTERS
Britain's Prime Minister Gordon Brown arrives for breakfast at the Munyonyo Resort during the Commonwealth Heads of Government Meeting in Kampala, Uganda. 24th November 2007.

martin rickett PRESS ASSOCIATION
Leader of the Conservative Party David Cameron walks through the Benchill area of Wythenshawe during his visit to Manchester whilst local youth Ryan Florence, 17, makes a gun gesture towards him. 22nd February 2007.

christopher furlong GETTY IMAGES
A lady enjoys the party atmosphere during the second day of the Grand National meeting at the Aintree Racecourse near Liverpool, England. The Friday is traditionally "Ladies Day" at the three-day National Hunt race meeting. 13th April 2007.

following spread

first prize: portraits
charles mcquillan PACEMAKER PRESS
The "Sky Blue" supporter The Dr. Ian Paisley pictured at the Ballymena Showground as he canvassed for votes before the Ballymena United versus Linfield Irish Cup game as the elections loomed for the big Ballymena man. 3rd March 2007.

graeme robertson

The Conservative Party Leader David Cameron buying some Blackpool rock from a shop on the pier during the party's conference. Blackpool, England. 30th September 2007.

tom stoddart GETTY IMAGES
News Corporation Chairman and CEO Rupert Murdoch photographed in his office at News International in Wapping, London, as he contemplates his bid to buy the Wall Street Journal. 15th June 2007.

following spread

matt dunham AP
British singer Amy Winehouse poses for photographs after an interview at a studio in north London. 16th February 2007.

jack hill
Singer and actor Billie Piper. London. 6th September 2007.

brian david stevens
The jazz singer and art critic George Melly with Molly Parkin on his last public appearance in London. 11th June 2007.

leon neal AGENCE FRANCE PRESSE
Singer Pete Doherty arrives at Thames Magistrates Court, London after being charged with four driving offences. 13th February 2007.

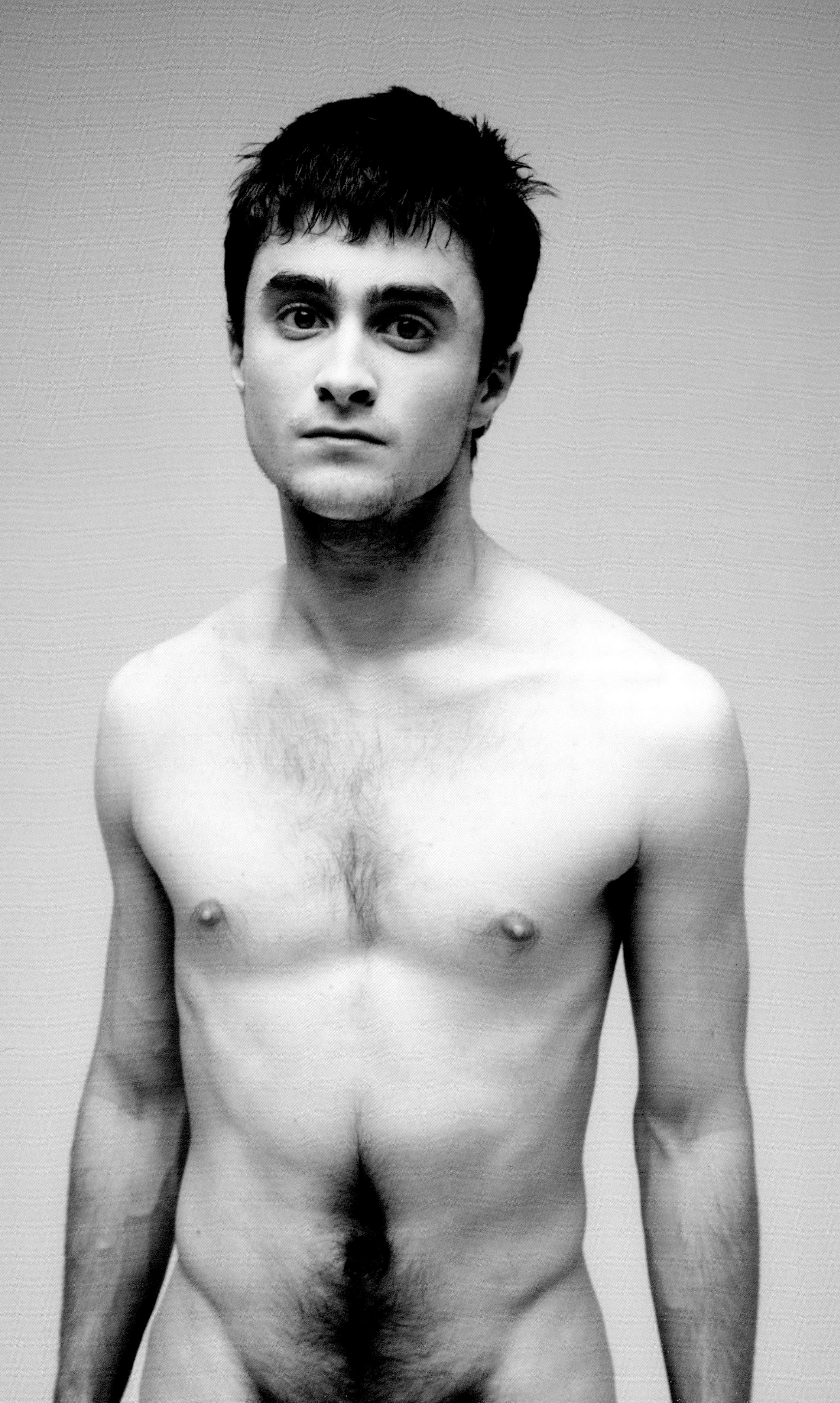

harry borden
Actor Daniel Radcliffe captured a week before his role in Equus. The play by Peter Shaffer tells the story of a psychiatrist who attempts to treat a young man who has a pathological religious and sexual fascination with horses. 18th January 2007.

gareth cattermole GETTY IMAGES
Actor Brad Pitt leaves by car after attending the premiere for the film "A Mighty Heart" at the Palais des Festivals during the 60th International Cannes Film Festival on May 21, 2007 in Cannes, France. 21st May 2007.

first prize: arts and entertainment

bryan o'brien THE IRISH TIMES
The dancer Kenneth Flak during rehearsals for his solo performance of "CYPI7" by the Canadian choreographer Andre Gingras. Sydney Opera House, Sydney, Australia. 1st August 2007.

harry borden
The band Radiohead photograph themselves.
21st November 2007.

ONEY ISLAND

felix clay

Day tripping families head home after spending the Fourth of July holiday at Coney Island. A New York seaside resort since the end of the Civil War, it is in the process of a $1.5 billion redevelopment and is set to close at the end of the summer season this year. Most of the area is due to be demolished before being replaced by ultra-modern, all-year-round theme park rides surrounded by luxury apartments, a Las Vegas style mega hotel and an indoor water park. 4th July 2007.

felix clay

A crowd watches a strong man try to hit a bell with the hammer. Coney Island. 4th July 2007.

felix clay

Children ride a roller coaster at Coney Island on the Fourth of July holiday. Coney Island. 4th July 2007.

felix clay

Stillwell Avenue subway station. Coney Island. 4th July 2007.

felix clay

Rides and rubbish at 1 a.m. Saturday morning, after a Friday night. Coney Island. 30th June 2007.

previous spread

richard cannon
Ronnie Corbett photographed at the Addington Palace Hotel, Addington, Surrey. 1st May 2007.

graeme robertson
The director, author and performer Neil Bartlett photographed in a studio in Brick Lane. Formerly the Artistic Director of the Lyric Theatre in Hammersmith, west London, he transformed the previously run-down venue into one of the most respected theatres in London. 15th April 2007.

nils jorgensen REX FEATURES
The artist Duane Hanson's piece "Traveller, 1988" exhibited at the National Gallery in London. Galleries in Bristol and Newcastle joined forces with the National Gallery to showcase brilliant new work in an exhibition entitled "Work, Rest & Play". 25th July 2007.

graeme robertson

Seduced: Art and Sex from Antiquity to Now. A major exhibition that focused on representations of sex from diverse eras and cultures staged at the Barbican Gallery, London, featuring over 300 works spanning 2000 years, it brought together Roman sculptures, Indian manuscripts, Japanese prints, Chinese watercolours, Renaissance and Baroque paintings and 19th century photography with modern and contemporary art. 21st November 2007.

charles mcquillan PACEMAKER PRESS
Stephen Lynch limbers up in an open training session for the media for his Ultimate Fighting Championship bout at Belfast's Odyssey Arena. 13th July 2007.

david bebber THE TIMES
The crowd at the Underage Festival in Victoria Park, London which claims to be the first music festival for 14 to 18 year olds. 9th August 2007.

john ferguson DAILY MIRROR
English National Ballet dancer Shevelle Dynott, 21, was discovered as a child when the 'Chance to Dance' charity visited his primary school in Brixton and he won a year of ballet lessons. In 1996, he became the first child from the scheme to win a place at the Royal Ballet School. Photographed on a South London council estate, as part of the 'Black Britannia' photography exhibition. 8th October 2007.

christopher furlong GETTY IMAGES
Figures from Anthony Gormley's art installation 'Another Place' stand in front of the turbines of the new Burbo Bank offshore wind farm in the mouth of the River Mersey near Liverpool, England, after their official inauguration. The offshore wind farm comprises 25 wind turbines and is situated in Liverpool Bay at the entrance to the River Mersey, about 4.0 miles from the Sefton coastline and is capable of generating up to 90 megawatts of clean, environmentally sustainable electricity: enough power for approximately 80,000 homes. 18th October 2007.

edmond terakopian
The Columbian artist Doris Salcedo's "Shibboleth" a subterranean chasm that stretches the length of the Turbine Hall at Tate Modern, Bankside, London. 8th October 2007.

stephen shepherd

From a personal project, taken in my grandmother's house. She is now 92 and I realised that the things I had seen around me and been familiar with for over 40 years may soon no longer be there. Looking around the house I saw that the décor had not really changed (except for the odd lick of paint) since the late 60s early 70s - even the carpet is reputed to be 40 years old. Unlike today where everyone is into clean décor, white walls and open spaces, every wall and surface of this house is filled with richly patterned fabrics, juxtaposed with brightly coloured walls, cushions and nik naks. This is obviously an older person's house and contains a different generation's ideas of decorating, colour and style. This, I felt, was worth recording, if only because of my own personal association with the house. 6th September 2007.

mike egerton PRESS ASSOCIATION
England's Jonny Wilkinson stands dejected at the end of the Rugby Union World Cup Final after his side lost to South Africa. Stade De France, Paris, France. 20th October 2007.

RUGBY
WORLD CUP
2007

first prize: news folio of the year

daniel berehulak GETTY IMAGES
The former English Football team coach Steve McClaren sits down in front of media before speaking at a press conference in St Albans, England after he was sacked by the FA when England failed to qualify for the Euro 2008 football championships, losing 2-3 to Croatia the day before. 22nd November 2007.

eamon ward
Flan McNamara, the scorekeeper at Cusack Park, Ennis, Ireland. Plans are underway to develop Cusack Park commercially and build a new GAA Grounds outside the town. 31st October 2007.

following spread

ryan pierse GETTY IMAGES
The McLaren Mercedes driver Fernando Alonso in action during Formula One testing at the Bahrain International Circuit in Sakhir. 1st March 2007.

carl de souza AGENCE FRANCE PRESS
A motocross rider tries to free his bike during the annual Weston beach race in Weston-Super-Mare, southwest England. 1,200 bikers competed in the event, which was celebrating its 25th anniversary. 21st October 2007.

marc aspland THE TIMES
Fernando Alonso swings round the first corner chicane on the opening lap of the Italian Grand Prix in Monza as Lewis Hamilton, in the McLaren Mercedes No. 2, gets sideways and airborne as he cuts across to reclaim second place. 9th September 2007.

paul gilham GETTY IMAGES
Lewis Hamilton, the McLaren Mercedes driver, celebrates after winning the Formula I Grand Prix of USA at the Indianapolis Motor Speedway. Indianapolis, Indiana. 17th June 2007.

eamon ward

The Irish boxer Mark Clancy awaits his debut fight against Andrew Hutchinson on on St. Patrick's Day. Madison Square Gardens, New York, USA. 17th March 2007.

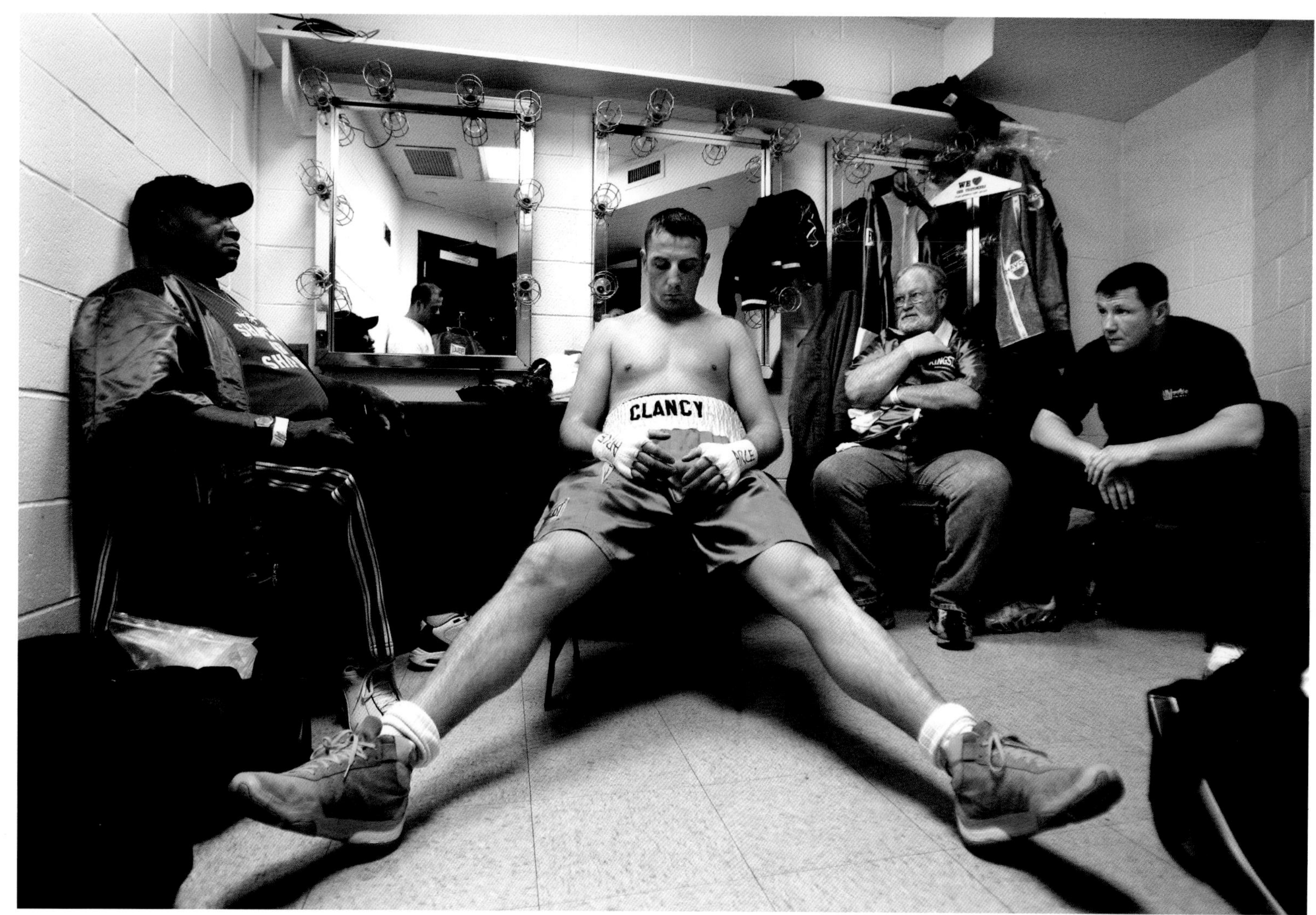

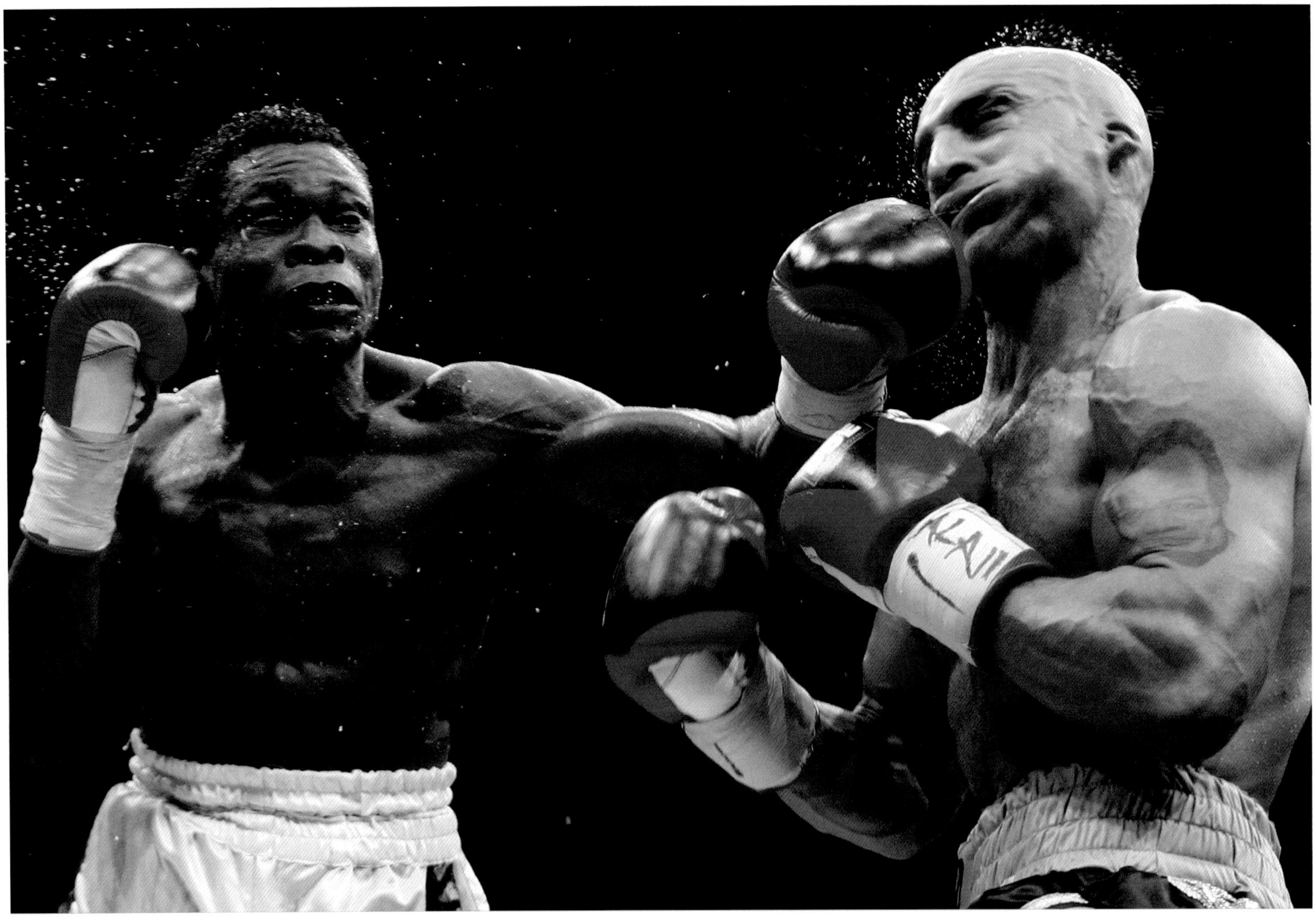

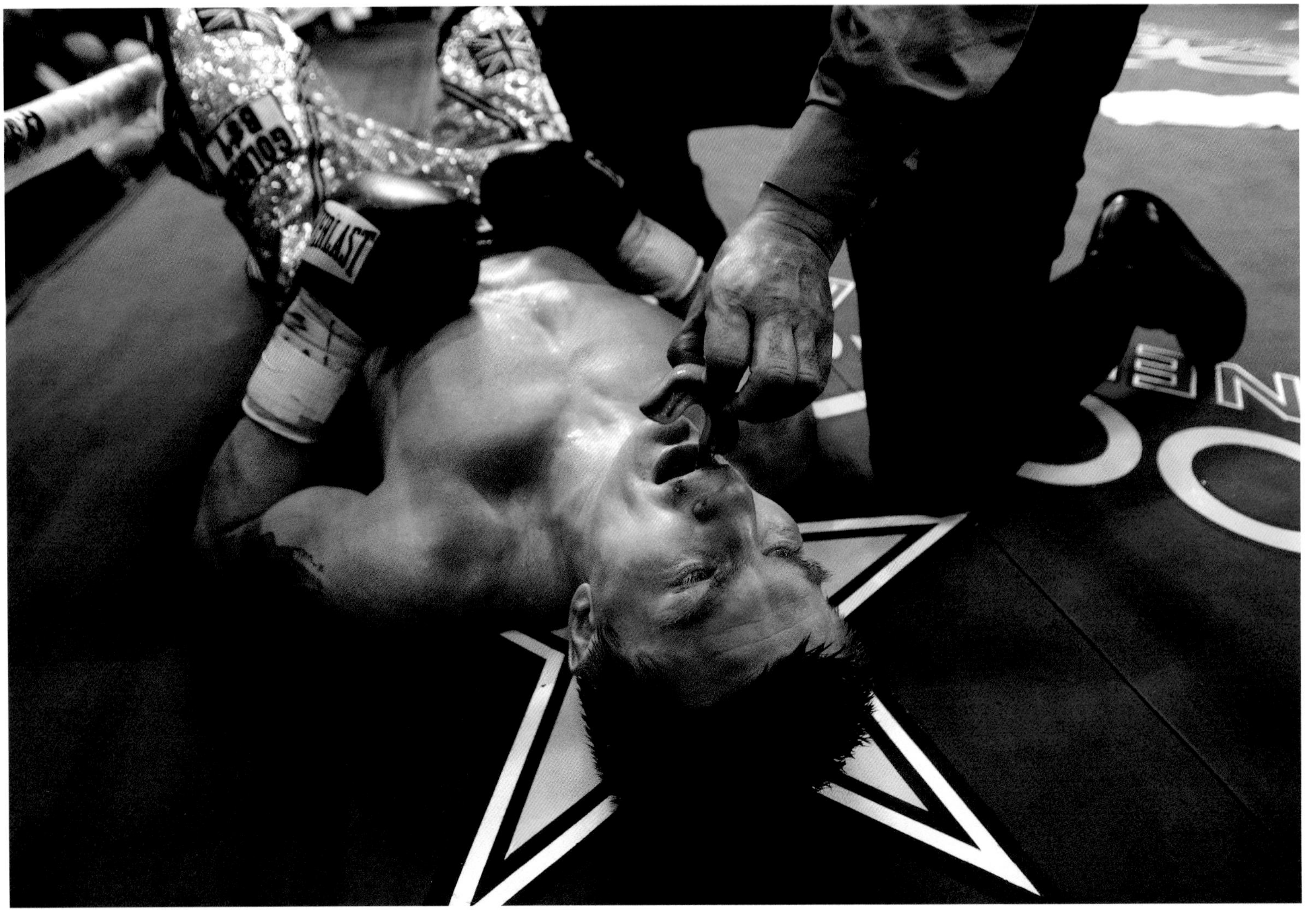

phil noble REUTERS
Ghanaian boxer Michael Gbenga catches Britain's Dean Francis off guard during their Commonwealth Light Heavyweight title fight in Bolton, England. 18th December 2007.

marc aspland THE TIMES
Referee Joe Cortez removes Ricky Hatton's gum shield after the boxer was knocked out in the 10th round of his fight with Floyd Mayweather Jr. at the MGM Grand Hotel Arena in Las Vegas, Nevada, USA. 8th December 2007.

mark robinson THE SUN
Ricky Hatton celebrates stopping Jose Luis Castillo in the 4th Round of their light welterweight fight at the Thomas and Mack Centre in Las Vegas, Nevada, USA. 23rd June 2007.

michael regan ACTION IMAGES
Spain's Rafael Nadal after winning his quarter final match during the French Open at Roland Garros, Paris, France. 6th June 2007.

nigel roddis REUTERS
Liverpool's Fernando Torres celebrates with teammates after scoring against Derby County during their English Premier League soccer match at Anfield in Liverpool, England. 1st September 2007.

julian finney GETTY IMAGES
Koo Kien Keat (L) and Tan Boon Heong of Malaysia celebrate after defeating Cai Yun and Fu Haifeng of China in the Men's Doubles final during the Yonex All England Open Badminton Championship at the NIA in Birmingham, England. 11th March 2007.

PROTON

tony o'brien ACTION IMAGES
Venus Williams dives for the ball during her fourth round match at The Championships, Wimbledon, London. 4th July 2007.

clive rose GETTY IMAGES
Rafael Nadal celebrates winning match point against Roger Federer during the Men's Singles Final of the French Open at Roland Garros, Paris, France. 10th June 2007.

phil noble REUTERS
Manchester United's Nani (TOP) celebrates after scoring during their English Premier League soccer match against Tottenham Hotspur in Manchester, England. 26th August 2007.

nigel roddis REUTERS
Liverpool's Lucas Leiva (L) challenges Newcastle United's Nicky Butt during their English Premier League soccer match at St James Park in Newcastle, England. 24th November 2007.

first prize: sports folio of the year
first prize: sports action

andy hooper DAILY MAIL
The Chelsea Captain John Terry is accidentally kicked in the face by the Arsenal player Abou Diaby during the Carling Cup Final. 25th February 2007.

first prize: sports specialist folio of the year

gareth copley PRESS ASSOCIATION
Sri Lanka's Lasith Malinga during their second One Day International match at Rangiri Dambulla Stadium, Dambulla, Sri Lanka. 4th October 2007

MAS

first prize: sports specialist folio of the year

gareth copley PRESS ASSOCIATION

Sri Lanka's Lasith Malinga tries to get a dog to leave the pitch during their third One Day International match at Rangiri Dambulla Stadium, Dambulla, Sri Lanka. 7th October 2007.

clive rose GETTY IMAGES
England's Jamie Dalrymple tries to make his ground during the Twenty20 International match between Australia and England, as Australia's Adam Gilchrist watches on. Sydney Cricket Ground, Sydney, Australia. 9th January 2007.

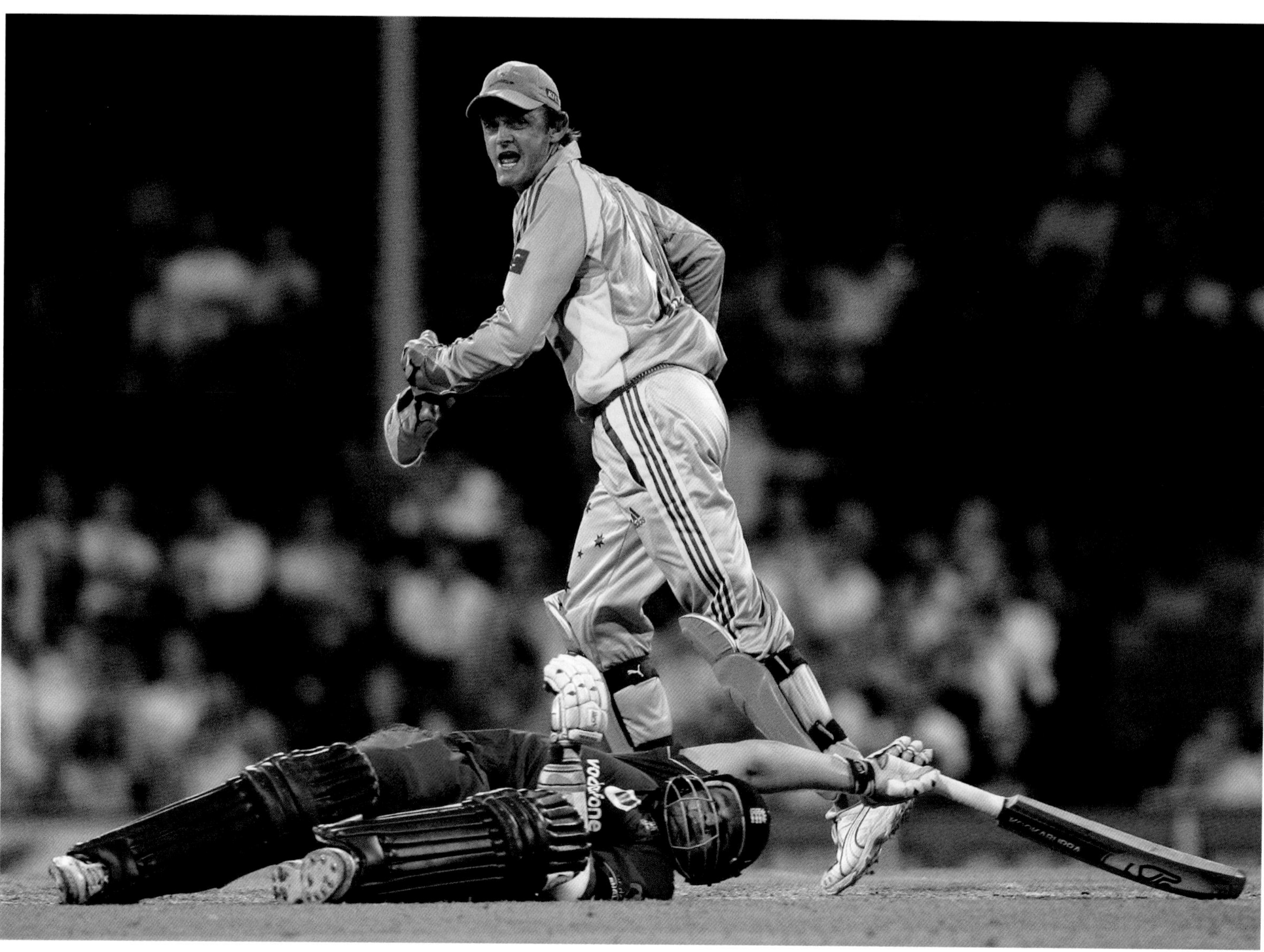

first prize: sports specialist folio of the year

gareth copley PRESS ASSOCIATION
England's Michael Vaughan during their warm up match at Colombo Cricket Club ground, Colombo, Sri Lanka. 21st November 2007.

first prize: sports specialist folio of the year

gareth copley PRESS ASSOCIATION
West Indies's Darren Sammy celebrates dismissing England's Alastair Cook for 60 runs during the npower Third Test match at Old Trafford, Manchester.
3rd January 2007.

first prize: sports specialist folio of the year

gareth copley PRESS ASSOCIATION
England's Monty Panesar watches as Australia captain Ricky Ponting (left) is run out by James Anderson during the second day of the fifth Test match at the SCG in Sydney, Australia.
7th June 2007.

first prize: sports specialist folio of the year

gareth copley PRESS ASSOCIATION
Sri Lankan fans watch their team's first One Day International match against England at Rangiri Dambulla International Stadium, Dambulla, Sri Lanka. 1st October 2007.

following spread

first prize: sports folio of the year
andy hooper DAILY MAIL
Night racing at Kempton Park, Middlesex, England.
6th December 2007.

richard heathcote GETTY IMAGES
The Frenchman Gregory Havret is drenched with champagne by Raphael Jacquelin following his victory in a play off with America's Phil Mickelson during the final round of The Barclays Scottish Open at Loch Lomond Golf Club, Luss, Scotland.
15th July 2007.

first prize: sports folio of the year

andy hooper DAILY MAIL
Didier Drogba celebrates scoring for Chelsea against Everton. 11th November 2007.

following spread

first prize: sports features
darren staples REUTERS
A competitor runs through fire during the "Tough Guy" event, a challenge involving running through an assault course of obstacles laid out over eight miles. Perton, South Staffordshire, England, 27th January 2008.

first prize: sports folio of the year
andy hooper DAILY MAIL
Tom Daley, the 13 year old diver from Plymouth, England, practicing for his 10m board event. He won both the Senior and Junior titles at the 2007 ASA National Championships and was awarded BBC Young Sports Personality of the Year. He is one of Britain's best hopes for the Beijing and London Olympics. 12th November 2007.

the press photographers year: photograph of the year
daniel berehulak GETTY IMAGES

first prize: live news

andrew parsons PA

first prize: news

peter macdiarmid GETTY IMAGES

first prize: features

nigel dickinson

first prize: portraits
charles mcquillan PACEMAKER F

first prize : photo essay david bebber THE TIMES

first prize : news folio of the year daniel berehulak GETTY IMAGES

first prize : sports specialist folio of the year gareth copley PRESS ASSOCIATION

first prize: sports folio of the year andy hooper DAILY MAIL

irst prize:
rts & entertainment
ryan o'brien THE IRISH TIMES

first prize:
sports action
andy hooper DAILY MAIL

first prize:
sports features
darren staples REUTERS

acknowledgements

The Press Photographer's Year would like to thank all the photographers who submitted photographs for the competition and for kindly allowing us to reproduce them in this book and at the accompanying exhibition.

The copyright for each of the photographs published in this book is held by the individual photographer with the exception of the following publications and agencies.

The Press Photographer's Year are very grateful to them for their permissions.

Action Images; 104, 108.
Agency France Presse; 64 top, 75 bottom, 98.
Associated Press; 20, 21, 74 top.
Daily Mail; 112, 120, 123, 125, 126-127.
Daily Mirror; 87.
Getty Images; 6, 22, 44, 56, 61, 69 right, 77, 88, 94, 96, 100, 106, 109, 115, 122, 126-127.
The Guardian; 10, 12 both, 13, 14, 51, 58, 65 bottom.
The Irish Times; 78, 126-127.
Pacemaker Press; 40, 70, 86 top, 126-127.
Press Association; 16, 42, 59, 60, 65 top, 66, 67, 69 left, 92, 113, 114, 116, 118, 119 both, 126-127.
Reuters; 68, 102 top, 105, 110, 111, 124, 126-127.
Rex Features; 84.
The Sun; 103.
The Times; 26, 28, 29 all, 64 bottom, 86 bottom, 99, 102 bottom.

The Press Photographer's Year would not have been possible without the generous support of Canon Cameras. We would like to thank Matt Beard at Canon UK for his dedication to the project.

We would also like to thank the following people for their time, their support and valuable assistance during The Press Photographer's Year.

the 2008 Jury
Clive Limpkin (Chairman)
Colin Davey
Graham Harrison
Eddie Mulholland
Abbie Trayler-Smith
Justin Sutcliffe

the 2008 Sports Jury
Bob Martin (Chairman)
Chris Cole

at TalkingPixels.co.uk
Tom Scott, James Crossett

at SMITH
Stuart Smith, Lesley Gilmour, Victoria Forrest

at the National Theatre
Nicholas Hytner, John Langley, Alison Chown
Hannah Wright

at Passavia & Euro Digital, Passau
Elmar Steubl, Michael Wallrapp, Sandra Kössl

at Loxley Colour, Glasgow
Christopher Kay, Robert Orr

a special vote of thanks must go to
Alastair Mackeown
Brian Murphy

thanks also to
Julien Allen, Carole Butcher, Melissa DeWitt, Graeme Fisher, Colin Hayward, Roger Hutchings, Nick Millen, Stuart Morcom, Donal Ogilvie, Victoria Routledge.

The accompanying exhibition held at the National Theatre's Lyttelton Foyer from 5th July to 30th August 2008 was designed by SMITH and printed by Loxley.

entrants for 2008

Bruce Adams
Jason Alden
Matthew Alexander
Roger Allen
Timothy Allen
Carol Allen Storey
Brian Anderson
Kirsty Anderson
Magnus Andersson
Julian Andrews
John Angerson
Frederic Aranda
Marc Aspland
Helen Atkinson
Richard Austin
David Azia
David Bagnall
Andrew Baker
Roger Bamber
Fraser Band
Jane Barlow
Tony Bartholomew
Barry Batchelor
David Bebber
Martin Beddall
Guy Bell
Louise Bellaers
Martin Bennett
Callum Bennetts
Daniel Berehulak
James Boardman
Silvia Boarini
Jon Bond
Harry Borden
Shaun Botterill
Stuart Boulton
Andrew Boyers
Jonathan Brady
Paula Bronstein
Sarah Lucy Brown
Philip Brown
Terence Bunch
Mark Bury
Jason Bye
Geoff Caddick
Andre Camara
Richard Cannon
Matt Cardy
Niall Carson
Angela Catlin
Gareth Cattermole
Darren Chaplin
Ian Chapman
Dan Charity
Wattie Cheung
Daniel Chung
Nobby Clark
Felix Clay
Philip Coburn
Len Copland
Gareth Copley
Carl Court
David Cowlard
Steve Cox
Michael Crabtree
Shaun Curry
Simon Dack
Brian David Stevens
Alan Davidson
David Davies
Kingsley Davis
Jason Dawson
Simon Dawson
Fabio De Paola
Carl de Souza
Peter Dench
Euan Denholm
Adrian Dennis
Anthony Devlin
Nigel Dickinson
Kieran Dodds
Kieran Doherty
Matt Dunham
Hazel Dunlop
Nic Dunlop
Richard Eaton
Mike Egerton
Stuart Emmerson
James Emmett
Jon Enoch
Jonathan Evans
John Ferguson
Luca Ferrari
Julian Finney
Adrian Fisk
Ian Forsyth
Lin Fou
Andrew Fox
Stuart Freedman
Sam Frost
Sam Furlong
Chris Furlong
Yoav Galai
James Galloway
Andy Garbutt
Javier Garcia
Adam Gasson
John Giles
Paul Gilham
Cate Gillon
Paul Glendell
Henning Gloystein
Martin Godwin
Anna Gordon
Charlie Gray
Kate Green
Claire Greenway
Stuart Griffiths
Spencer Griffiths
Laurence Griffiths
Ben Gurr
Rosie Hallam
Paul Harding
Rebecca Harley
Brian Harris
Richard Heathcote
Scott Heavey
Maros Herc
Sean Hernon
Tom Hevezi
Mike Hewitt
Andrew Higgins
Jack Hill
Stephen Hird
David Hoffman
David Hogan
Andy Hooper
Scott Hornby
Michael Hughes
Richard Humphries
Susannah Ireland
Christopher Ison
Christopher Jackson
Tom Jenkins
Bob Johns
Nils Jorgensen
Irina Kalashnikova
Frantzesco Kangaris
Liz Kearsley
Clare Kendall
Eddie Keogh
Ady Kerry
Roy Kilcullen
Glyn Kirk
Matthew Kirwan
Dan Kitwood
David Klein
Ash Knotek
Richard Lea-Hair
Will Leach
Colm Lenaghan
Amit Lennon
Bryn Lennon
David Levene
Geraint Lewis
Dominic Lipinski
Alex Livesey
Mikal Ludlow
Michael Lusmore
Daniel Lynch
Peter Macdiarmid
Alex Macnaughton
Ian MacNicol
Toby Madden
Thomas Main
David Maitland
Brandon Malone
Mike Marsland
Dylan Martinez
Daniel Martino
Clive Mason
Dan Matthams
James McCauley
Andrew McConnell
Leon McGowran
John D. McHugh
Cathal McNaughton
Colin McPherson
Charles McQuillan
Catherine Mead
Colin Mearns
Toby Melville
Dustin Michailovs
John Millard
Stuart Miller
Andrew Milligan
Jane Mingay
Jeff Mitchell
Clara Molden
Mimi Mollica
Mike Moore
Jeff Moore
Peter Muhly
Max Mumby
Brendan Murphy
Donna Murray
Rebecca Naden
Max Nash
Leon Neal
Paul Nicholls
Peter Nicholls
Ian Nicholson
Phil Noble
Bryan O'Brien
Tony O'Brien
Jason O'Brien
Heathcliff O'Malley
Bradley Ormesher
Jeff Overs
David Parry
Steve Parsons
Andrew Parsons
Steven Paston
Teri Pengilley
Dan Phillips
Ryan Pierse
Tom Pilston
Mark Pinder
Lefteris Pitarakis
Christopher Pledger
Suzanne Plunkett
Richard Pohle
Geoff Pugh
Chris Radburn
Ben Radford
Lucy Ray
Nick Ray
Carl Recine
Michael Regan
Stefan Reimschuessel
Val Reynolds Brown
Martin Rickett
Steve Roberts
Gary Roberts
Graeme Robertson
Mark Robinson
Nigel Roddis
Angeles Rodenas
Paul Rogers
Clive Rose
Stefan Rousseau
Russell Sach
Peter Sandground
Oli Scarff
Georgie Scott
Tom Scott
Jeremy Selwyn
Ahikam Seri
Stephen Shepherd
Martin Shields
Dave Shopland
John Sibley
David Silverman
Julian Simmonds
Jamie Simpson
Derek Simpson
Christian Sinibaldi
David Sleator
Guy Smallman
Tim Smith
Sean Smith
Matt Sprake
Simon Stacpoole
Benjamin Stansall
Darren Staples
Wayne Starr
Michael Steele
Mark Stewart
Tom Stoddart
Bettina Strenske
Akira Suemori
Jonathan Super
Sang Tan
Ray Tang
Edmond Terakopian
Andrew Testa
Lee Thompson
Mark Thompson
Ed Thompson
Allan Titmuss
Chris Tofalos
Felipe Trueba Garcia
Mary Turner
Marc Turner
Neil Turner
Carmen Valino
Toby Vandevelde
Eva Vermandel
James Veysey
Rui Vieira
Bruno Vincent
Richard Wainwright
Brad Wakefield
Stuart Walker
Howard Walker
Michael Walter
Ian Walton
Eamon Ward
Lenny Warren
Neil Watcyn-Palmer
Zak Waters
Andy Weekes
Lewis Whyld
Kirsty Wigglesworth
Jim Wileman
Sarah Williams
Les Wilson
Carsten Windhorst
William Wintercross
Mark Wohlwender
Matt Writtle
Lucy Young
Chris Young
Ronen Zvulun